Japan is an archipelago of several thousand islands. It extends 2,366 miles in an arc off the eastern coast of Asia. Its area is 145,870 square miles, slightly smaller than California. There are four main islands: Hokkaido, Honshu, Shikoku, and Kyushu.

Because of its length, Japan's climate ranges from northern, with long, snowy winters, to temperate, with hot, humid summers.

About 75% of Japan's territory is mountainous. The highest mountain, Mt. Fuji (12,328 feet) is one of Japan's many dormant volcanoes. Much of Japan is covered with forest.

Japan's 126 million people live on just ten percent of the land. Flat plains on each of the major islands are densely populated. The capital Tokyo, is one of the world's largest cities, with more than eight million people.

Floating Lanterns and Golden Shrines

Celebrating Japanese Festivals

Text by Rena Krasno

Illustrations by Toru Sugita

Pacific View Press

Berkeley, California

To my dear friend Nobuko Eisenberg, in memory of her daughter, Elfriede (Yuki) —R.K.

To my nephew, Rin Hiwatashi—T.S.

This book would not have been possible without the generous assistance of the following friends and associates: Nobuko Eisenberg, Noriko Kumoi Ray, Cota Yabut, Yoko Woodsen, Maiko R. Behr, Florence Hongo, Miyako Sueyoshi and the staff of the Western Addition Branch of the San Francisco Public Library.

Credits:
Page 27, haiku, reprinted from Edward Seidensticker, Japan (New York: Time, Inc., 1961).
Page 44, "The Sakura Song," translation courtesy of Noriko Kumoi Ray.

Library of Congress Catalog Card Number: LC 99-047162
ISBN 1-881896-21-8

Printed in China by Twin Age Limited

Library of Congress Cataloging-in-Publication Data
Krasno, Rena, 1923–
     Floating lanterns and golden shrines : celebrating Japanese festivals / text by Rena Krasno ; illustrated by Toru Sugita.
         p. cm.
     Includes index.
     Summary: Describes a year of special celebrations in Japan, with historical and cultural information, including recipes, crafts, and legends.
     ISBN 1-881896-21-8 (alk.paper)
     1. Festivals—Japan—Juvenile literature. 2. Japan—Social life and customs—Juvenile literature. 3. Japan—History—Juvenile literature. [1. Festivals—Japan. 2. Holidays—Japan. 3. Japan—Social life and customs.] I. Sugita, Toru, ill. II. Title.
     GT4884.A2 K7 2000
394.26952—dc 21
                               99-047162

Contents

Welcome! Yokoso!

Yokoso
Welcome

Wasshoi! Wasshoi! The chanting grows louder. A procession moves slowly up the street. Muscular young men and boys crowd together, struggling to carry a golden **mikoshi** (shrine) on their shoulders. The mikoshi, from a nearby **Shinto** shrine, is very heavy. It weighs more than a ton. The men wear **happi** (short cotton jackets held with a sash). White **hachi maki** (headbands) around their foreheads keep the sweat from their eyes. Suddenly, the men toss the shrine up, into the air. They catch it as it drops. Spectators laugh and applaud. Children shriek. Up goes the shrine again! Down it comes and is grabbed by strong hands. When the men tire, others reach in to take a turn. Crowds line the sidewalks. There are men in suits, women wearing the latest styles, kids in school uniforms, elderly women dressed in **kimono**. Bright neon signs advertise autos, electronic games, hamburgers.

Japan is a land of the old and the new. The people have been one people, Japanese, for more than 2,000 years. They share similar beliefs and ways of doing things, and speak the same language. Long ago they worshipped the spirits of the mountains, trees, and streams. Farmers sought help from the gods of rain, fishermen from the gods of the sea. Since ancient times they also learned from other people, absorbing ideas from Asia and the West, changing them to suit Japanese needs.

Today Japan is one of the world's most modern, prosperous nations. But its people still honor the traditions of their religions. They celebrate their history. They cherish the natural wonders of their beautiful, rugged islands. In Japan, people love festivals. There are festivals to observe the change of seasons, festivals for children and for ancestors, festivals to welcome good spirits, festivals to chase off bad ones. Sometimes people just celebrate being Japanese, being with each other. Together, thousands gaze at cherry blossoms in a Tokyo park, or stand quietly on a frosty midnight as temple bells slowly toll in the New Year.

Come join them. You'll be welcome! **Yokoso!**

The First Japanese People

Who were the first Japanese people? We know Ice Age hunters roamed Japan more than 30,000 years ago, when Japan was part of the Korean peninsula. After the Ice Age ended and the rising sea created the Japanese islands, small tribes of nomads were living here. These people fished, hunted, and gathered plants. They also made pottery. Today we call them the **Jomon**, ("cord") because of the designs on their pottery. Archeologists have learned a little about their life. The Jomon relied on the forests and ocean for what they needed. They probably lived and worked together in small family groups. They settled in small villages. Centuries passed.

Meanwhile, life in other parts of Asia was becoming much more complex. People learned to farm, and to mine for metal and form it into tools and weapons. They made boats and carts. In China they learned to grow silkworms and weave silk cloth. They developed a written language and built cities. Their leaders lived in large palaces, ruled many people, and organized armies. We can guess that some intrepid travelers from Asia may have ventured to the Japanese islands. But there are no signs that their ideas or skills changed Jomon life.

Finally, around 300 B.C. something big happened. New people crossed the sea from the Korean Peninsula. These people could make tools and weapons from iron and bronze. They knew farming, and, especially, how to grow large crops of rice. They spoke a different language and had their own religious ideas. Their society was organized into clans, large groups of people who were only distantly related.

No one knows just what happened next, but everything changed very rapidly. Within several hundred years, Japan was a land of settled rice growers who were organized by clans, spoke a common language, and believed in gods called **kami**. Japan was now Japan.

Today, over 99% of Japan's people are ethnically Japanese. The Ainu people, who live on the northern island of Hokkaido, are Japan's only indigenous minority. No one knows their origins. Their ancestors may have crossed from Asia after the Japanese islands formed. Or they may be descended from the Jomon people. Modern science may eventually find the answer. About .5% of Japan's people are ethnic Koreans, whose families emigrated to Japan in the early twentieth century.

Amaterasu, the Sun Goddess

The oldest religion in Japan is Shinto, which means "way of the gods." The story of the Sun Goddess tells how humans and nature were created by the same gods, the kami. Shinto teaches that every mountain, river, tree, and rock has its own guardian spirit. People must respect nature.

The ideas and stories of Shinto were not written down until after Buddhism had become Japan's official religion in the seventh century, so today Shinto includes many Buddhist and Confucian ideas.

For centuries, the emperors of Japan claimed to be directly descended from the grandson of Amaterasu, the Sun Goddess.

Mukashi, mukashi, a long, long time ago, there was no order in the world. There were no people and no land, only water, spirits, and gods. Then one day heaven and earth parted. A male god, Izanagi, and a female god, Izanami, heard the thundering command: "Create the sacred islands of Japan!"

Izanagi and Izanami stood on the Floating Bridge of Heaven over an immense ocean. Together they plunged a long jeweled spear deep into the salt water.

They stirred hard until large drops thickened, slid off the spear, and became the islands of Japan.

Then Izanagi and Izanami began to create new gods. After Izanami gave birth to her last god, she retired to the World of Death. Izanagi continued creation alone. Many new gods were born from his sword and clothing.

The two most powerful were Amaterasu, the Sun Goddess, and her brother, Susanowo, the God of Force. They crunched their great jewel-studded swords into bits which changed into more gods. These gods became the heads of clans who were the ancestors of the Japanese people.

The God of Force did not want to share power with his sister. He pounded a hole through the Roof of Heaven over her head. Furious, the Sun Goddess swept into a deep cave taking all earthly light away with her.

"We need our light back!" moaned the other gods as they stumbled in the dark. Eight hundred gathered and decided on a plan.

They ordered pure iron from the Heavenly Metal Mountains to be forged into a mirror. The Grand Jeweler also made an eight-foot-long necklace of 500 precious stones, which the gods hung around the frame of the mirror. Then they laughed with joy.

"Why are they laughing?" the Sun Goddess wondered. Peeking out, she saw the magnificent mirror and jewels. She could not resist stepping out for a closer look. In a flash, light returned to the universe.

The God of Force was banished from heaven. The Sun Goddess never forgave him. She gave her favorite grandson the mirror and string of jewels. He became the ruler of Japan. Although the God of Force and his family continued war against the Sun Goddess's grandson and his close relatives, they finally had to admit defeat.

Setsubun

Bean-Throwing Festival

*The date of **Setsubun** (February 3 or 4) is determined by the Chinese calender adopted by Japan around 500 A.D. This calendar has four seasons and 24 divisions. Setsubun means the end of a season, the time it passes on to the next. So there are four setsubun in a year. The most celebrated setsubun is the end of winter. This is the time for **mamemaki**, bean-throwing.*

"**Oni-wa soto!**" Devils out! Handfuls of roasted **mame**, soybeans, fly out the front door of the house.

"**Fuku-wa uchi!**" Good luck into the house! More soybeans, this time thrown in from outside.

Tomorrow is **Risshun**, the first day of spring. Tonight it is Setsubun, the end of winter. Mamemaki, bean-throwing, is such fun! Kids are running around all over the house. Some are making scary faces pretending to be evil goblins. Others are wearing **oni**, devil masks that came with the packages of soybeans. Oh how they scream, while other kids chase them and pelt them with beans!

Want to be lucky? Eat one bean for every year of your life, plus one extra one for the coming year.

What smells so bad? The family has hung the heads of grilled sardines outside the front door to keep the devils away. They hope the oni will think: "We can't go into this house. It really stinks!"

The next day (by now it's Risshun) offers a chance to see famous athletes, movie stars, and local heroes who visit Buddhist temples and Shinto shrines. Outside, many people are waiting. . . . At last, here come the celebrities! They fling handfuls of mame to the crowd shouting:

"Good luck! Good luck!"

Hundreds of eager hands stretch out. They try to catch at least one bean. It's a lucky charm. "I got two! I got two!" a little girl cries excitedly.

おにはそと

Oni wa Soto!
Devils Out!

Sacred Rice

Rice became sacred to the Japanese. They believed it to be the food of gods. To this day, when a new emperor is enthroned, freshly harvested rice is offered to the God of Heaven and Earth. Every summer, the emperor plants the first rice sprouts in a paddy on his palace grounds. This ceremony is called **otaue.** And Japanese children are told the story of Otake, a young cook who was so careful not to waste a single grain of rice that one day a silver halo of light appeared over her rice strainer.

The Japanese eat rice so often that their word for a meal is **gohan,** which means "steamed rice." Breakfast is called **asa gohan** (morning rice), lunch is **hiru gohan** (noon rice), and dinner is **yu gohan** (evening rice). On happy occasions such as birthdays, graduation, and holidays, mothers prepare red rice, which is sweet (glutinous) rice steamed with red beans. Hot rice is usually accompanied by fish, vegetables, chicken, or meat.

In Japan, people eat with short chopsticks called **hashi.** Rice is usually served in small bowls. You hold your rice bowl close to your face, with three fingers under the bottom, and the thumb on the upper rim. The rice is rather sticky and easy to eat with hashi.

Lacquerware

Rice is sometimes served in a lacquerware bowl. Lacquer is a sticky resin from the lac tree, a kind of sumac. These trees also grow in China, India, and Burma. Many coats of lacquer are applied to bowls, boxes, trays, and furniture. The result is a beautiful, lustrous, long-lasting surface. The art of lacquer was brought from China to Japan, but Japanese artists developed their own shapes, designs, and colors. Japanese lacquerware is reddish brown, black, or gold.

Onigiri—A Rice Snack

Japanese children love these cold rice snacks. They're handy for school lunch and picnics.

  1 cup short grain rice

  1¼ cups cold water

  2 teaspoons black sesame seeds

1. Put the rice in a deep pot that has a tight-fitting lid. Cover the grains with water, stir with one hand. Drain. Repeat 3 or 4 times until the water is quite clear.
2. Add the cold water and bring to a boil. Turn the heat to very low, cover the pot, cook for 20 minutes, or until water is absorbed. Take pot off the heat, and let stand, still covered, for 10 minutes. Then fluff the rice with a fork.
3. While rice is cooking, toast the sesame seeds in oven at 350° for 5 minutes, or in a frying pan on stove at medium heat for 2 minutes. Stir often.

Moisten hands. Take a small handful of rice, about 2 tablespoons. Put both hands together around the rice and press firmly against each other. Shape the rice into a pyramid. Try to make the **onigiri** neat and symmetrical. Touch the sesame seed gently with the rice pyramid so that the seeds stick to all sides. Repeat until all the boiled rice is used. Eat!

Variation: Musubi

These snacks have a tart, salty surprise.

  Rice as above

  1 bottle **ume** (salty pickled plums)

  1 package **nori** (dried seaweed sheets, as for **sushi**)

Cook rice as for onigiri and shape into balls. With scissors, cut nori into strips about an inch wide and 4 inches long. Bury an ume in the center of each rice ball. Wrap a strip of nori around each ball. Moisten the end of the nori with a wet finger to help it stick closed. Eat!

Believers of Shinto build shrines for their gods among trees, in quiet places. The entrance to the shrine is a bright red gate called **torii**. Before entering a sacred shrine, Japanese rinse their mouths and pour water over their hands to clean and purify themselves.

In Japanese, the word for "beauty" and "clean" is the same—**kirei**. Japanese enjoy a bath in a deep tub, **furo**. Before stepping into the furo, people wash themselves until they are clean. Then they sit in the tub with hot water up to their neck and relax. Often several people soak together. Natural hot-spring furo are very popular.

Momo Taro, the Peach Boy

In Japan there are kami, gods, and there are also oni, evil spirits. Every child in Japan knows the story of Momo Taro and some wicked oni devils. Here is one version.

Long ago, a woodcutter lived in a forest with his loyal wife. There was only one dark cloud in their life: they had no children. One day, the woman was washing clothes in the river when she saw a huge peach floating toward her. It looked delicious. Quickly she grabbed it and took it home.

After dinner, when the woodcutter took a sharp knife to slice the peach, he heard a tiny voice: "Careful! Careful! Don't hurt me!" Who was inside the fruit? The man carefully broke it open. A little boy jumped out. They named him Momo Taro, which means Peach Boy in Japanese.

Momo Taro was a good and loving son. When he grew older, wicked devils called oni came to terrorize the villagers. They had thick, straight, bushy hair, sharp horns, bulging eyes, huge fangs, and curved claws. The oni stole the villagers' possessions and kidnapped babies. The only way to make the oni powerless was to cut off their horns, but who would dare try?

Brave Momo Taro decided to fight the oni. His worried mother gave him three big onigiri to take along—his favorite snack. His father bought him a sword and a warrior's armor, and off he went.

As Momo Taro climbed up the oni's mountain, a skinny dog followed him. Momo Taro fed him one onigiri and the grateful animal stayed at his side. Later, a monkey tried to steal an onigiri. He hissed loudly at the dog. Momo Taro gave the monkey an onigiri and made him promise to behave. Then a hungry pheasant landed on the boy's shoulder, so the kind young-ster gave him his very last onigiri. Now he had no food left for himself, but hunger would not stop him.

Finally, there stood the oni's castle, surrounded by a huge thick wall with an enormous locked gate. Up flew the pheasant, flapping his wings wildly and making ear-piercing cries. The dog and the monkey banged loudly at the gate shouting:

"Our powerful Lord, Momo Taro-san, is here with all his soldiers! Beware! Beware!"

When the terrified oni opened the gate to peek out, the pheasant swooped on their heads and pecked their eyes, the dog dashed in and bit them, and the monkey pulled their hair. Quickly, Momo Taro rushed at the devils and chopped off their horns with his sword. The oni escaped to the edge of the cliffs, fell off, and were never seen again!

Then Momo Taro took home on a cart everything the oni had stolen. He returned the villagers' babies and their possessions. His parents were very proud of him. The dog, the monkey, and the pheasant remained good friends and were never, never hungry again.

Obon

Every year from August 13 to August 16, millions of Japanese celebrate the Obon festival. They honor the spirits of their dead ancestors who return for a short visit to the world of the living. Many businesses close and people go on summer vacation. Employers hand out bonuses to workers. Businesses might give gifts to special customers and students might give something to teachers.

Families are gathering in the square. It's hot. Several men struggle to lug a huge **taiko** drum up onto a high **yagura** (a platform made of bamboo and wood). Vendors offer tempting mounds of shaved ice with colorful syrup. Children excitedly patrol the stalls, examining souvenirs and folk toys.

Here are crickets for sale in tiny bamboo cages! Take one home, hang it under your roof and listen to its cheerful chirping. Then at the end of August, release it, with a good-by song.

Boom! Boom! Boom! The drummers begin. Rhythm fills the square. A group of women begins to dance the **bon-odori.** The dance steps are simple but graceful. Now others—men and women, boys and girls—join in. Many wear cotton **yukata**, the summer **kimono**. People dance in a wide circle around the yagura. A second circle forms, then a third. Bamboo flutes and folk singers add to the cheerful din.

Before the festival, people have cleaned family graves. They have swept, pulled weeds, watered plants, and brought fresh flowers.

On the first night of the festival, families return to the cemetery. It is dark. Everyone carries a white lantern with a glowing candle inside it to show the spirits the way home. Burning incense sticks lend a spicy smell. Spooky? Nobody is afraid. The spirits will not hurt them. Back home, families will eat a festive dinner. They remember to prepare the favorite foods of their dead relatives, especially those who passed away recently.

On the last night of the festival, families with lighted lanterns will guide the spirits back to cemeteries, to the Celestial World of Darkness. People living near a river, lake, or sea, send the spirits away on tiny boats. Some bear the name of an ancestor written by a priest. Their miniature lanterns flicker like fireflies in the dark.

Bon Odori
Bon Dancing

Ideas From China

Most Japanese have two altars in their homes: a Shinto one for the gods and a Buddhist one for the family ancestors. They follow a mixture of both religions. They marry the Shinto way. When they die, they are cremated and Buddhist prayers are said. Each family prays for the spirits of their dead ancestors. Honoring one's ancestors is part of both Shinto and Buddhist practice in Japan.

Confucius was a Chinese philosopher in the fourth century B.C. He believed that there was a certain order to the universe. Peace and prosperity occurred when people followed certain rules, according to their place in the social order. His ideas were soon adopted by Chinese rulers. Confucianism is not a religion, but these ideas about how to behave have influenced people and governments in Asia for more than 2,000 years.

Farmers need land, so clans often fought over territory in old Japan. Gradually, one group of clans, the Yamato, controlled southern Japan. And Japan was no longer isolated from the rest of Asia. It was a great time for Japanese culture. From China via Korea came many new ideas about art, music, literature, and technology. They took root, grew, and changed to fit what Japan needed. Confucian scholars taught how important it was to be educated and to honor one's parents. The first Buddhist scriptures arrived. In the sixth century A.D., Japanese scholars discovered they could use Chinese characters to write Japanese. Now Japan had a written language. Around 500 A.D. the Yamato kings, copying Korean ideas, gave military titles and jobs to clan leaders, creating a military aristocracy. (This aristocracy became the most powerful group in Japan. Its power lasted more than 1,400 years.) Soon the Yamato had trouble controlling the other clans. So in the seventh century they formed a Chinese-style empire. They wrote a constitution based on Confucian principles. They replaced their "king" with an emperor who claimed he was a descendant of the Sun God and ruled by the will of heaven. He had absolute authority. They created a bureaucracy of government officials to run the entire country. Japan adopted the Chinese calendar and Buddhism became its official religion.

Buddhism

Buddha (Siddhartha Guatama) was an Indian philosopher who lived during the fifth century B.C. Buddha did not talk about gods. He taught that people could achieve salvation by seeking truth and practicing tolerance and respect. His teachings spread to China, and eventually throughout Asia. As time went on, Buddha's followers developed many ways of interpreting his ideas.

In Japan, some Buddhists sought enlightenment through intense study, others through art and beauty, and yet others through meditation. At first, only the court nobility had the time and education to study and practice Buddhism. Later on, other Buddhist sects taught that salvation could be reached by praying and devotions. Then ordinary people could also participate. Buddhism became a popular religion.

The Legend of Daruma

About 1,500 years ago, Daruma was born in India to a noble family. Even as a boy, he was not interested in things money could buy. He wanted to understand the human soul. Later he left his parents to study with a famous Buddhist teacher. Before he died, the holy man asked Daruma to take his place. He accepted and became famous for his wisdom.

When Daruma was 100 years old, he decided to take a message to the Chinese people:

"Look inside your hearts and lead good lives."

In China, Emperor Wu called Daruma to his palace. He expected words of praise from Daruma because he had built many Buddhist temples.

"Do you think I am a worthy man?" the emperor asked.

"No," Daruma replied.

The emperor did not understand that giving money for temples and statues was not what counted. What mattered was what kind of human being you were.

Daruma then travelled deeper into China till he reached a cave near a Buddhist temple. There he sat for nine years thinking about nature, human beings, and the universe.

When he finally decided to get up, he could not stand. His legs had fallen off! His arms also had withered.

The real Daruma was Bodhidharma, who brought the Zen school of Buddhism from India to China.

Today there are more than 100 Buddhist sects and 80,000 Buddhist temples in Japan. Columns and heavy gates are at the temple entrance. The roofs are high and curved. Some Japanese believe that this will make evil devils slip off and be killed.

Daruma Dolls

Daruma dolls have no arms and no legs. They can be made of wood, clay, rock, or papiér-mâché, and they come in all sizes. All have a round weighted bottom that makes them pop back up when you push them down. They teach that a person who falls down can always come up again, and should never give up.

Daruma dolls are usually painted red, except for their faces, which are white with black lines. They never smile. Their eyes are very large and very black. Some Daruma dolls have blank circles for eyes. They are wish dolls. Paint one eye while making a wish. Paint the second one when your wish comes true. Politicians sometimes have Daruma dolls in their offices. They paint the second eye when they get elected.

Japanese Writing

The first Japanese novel was written in **hiragana.** When Lady Murasaki Shikibu wrote the *Tale of Genji* in the eleventh century, women weren't given the education needed to write in **kanji.** Women writers of the day used hiragana, and it was often called "women's writing."

Japanese is written by mixing Chinese characters, called **kanji** and two alphabets. Each kanji stands for an idea. Kanji was difficult to learn, and didn't really reflect how people talked, so around the ninth century Japanese scholars developed two new alphabets—**hiragana** and **katakana**—based on the sound of Japanese. These scripts each have 46 symbols. Each symbol stands for a sound. Today Japanese often use kanji, hiragana, and katakana in the same text. Kanji is used for ideas and nouns and verbs. Hiragana is used for verb endings and other parts of speech. Hiragana symbols have mostly curved lines. Katakana is used mainly for foreign words and names, and sounds, and has straight lines.

Here is an example: Notice how the word order is very different from English. "Wa" is a part of speech showing that "kazoku" is the subject.

The family is flying to Paris this summer.

kanji	*hiragana*	*hiragana*	*kanji*
家族	は	この	夏
Kazoku	wa	kono	natsu
Family		this	summer

hiragana	*katakana*	*hiragana*	*kanji and hiragana combined*
に	パリ	へ	行きます
ni	Paris	e	ikimasu
in	Paris	to	is going

Today there are 50,000 kanji characters in Japanese, but only about 2,000 are used regularly. Children learn 1,850 kanji by the end of middle school. And they must also learn hiragana and katakana. About 50% of the words in newpapers are written with kanji, and the rest with hiragana and katakana.

Traditional Japanese writing is printed in vertical lines beginning at the top right side of the page. Books are read from right to left. Today Japanese writing is often done from left to right across the page, like English writing.

The Daruma Staring Game

Try this. Two children stand facing each other and chant together:

Daruma-san, Daruma-san   Daruma-san, Daruma-san

Let's play a staring game.   Niramekko shimasho

The one who laughs loses.   Warau to make yo.

They finish chanting, fold their arms, look at each other daringly and say: "A-pupu! Go!" Then both children puff up their cheeks, squint their eyes and twist their mouths making funny faces. The first one to laugh loses the game.

In Japan you always add a polite word after the name of a person. If a child's name is Yuki, you say Yuki-**chan**. **San** follows a man's or woman's family name. Sometimes when a person is very important or respected, **sama** is added after the family name. Japanese say their family name first and their given name last. In the past only samurai and important families had family names. In the nineteenth century, farmers, merchants, and other commoners were allowed to choose a family name.

Drums

The rhythm of drums has been heard in Japanese festivals and religious ceremonies for hundreds of years. Japanese drums are handmade of wood, preferably from a section of a large tree. They come in different sizes. The largest are held vertically on a stand, and played by two people. In Japanese tradition, drums have their own spirit. Today, **taiko** (fat drum), usually refers to a style of ensemble drumming with fast, powerful rhythms. It is extremely popular, with over 4,000 performing groups in Japan and 150 in North America. Like martial arts, taiko drumming can be a way of life, too. In order to unite their spirits with those of the drum, taiko performers often live communally, do physical training (especially running) together, and study their art at taiko **dojo** (studios).

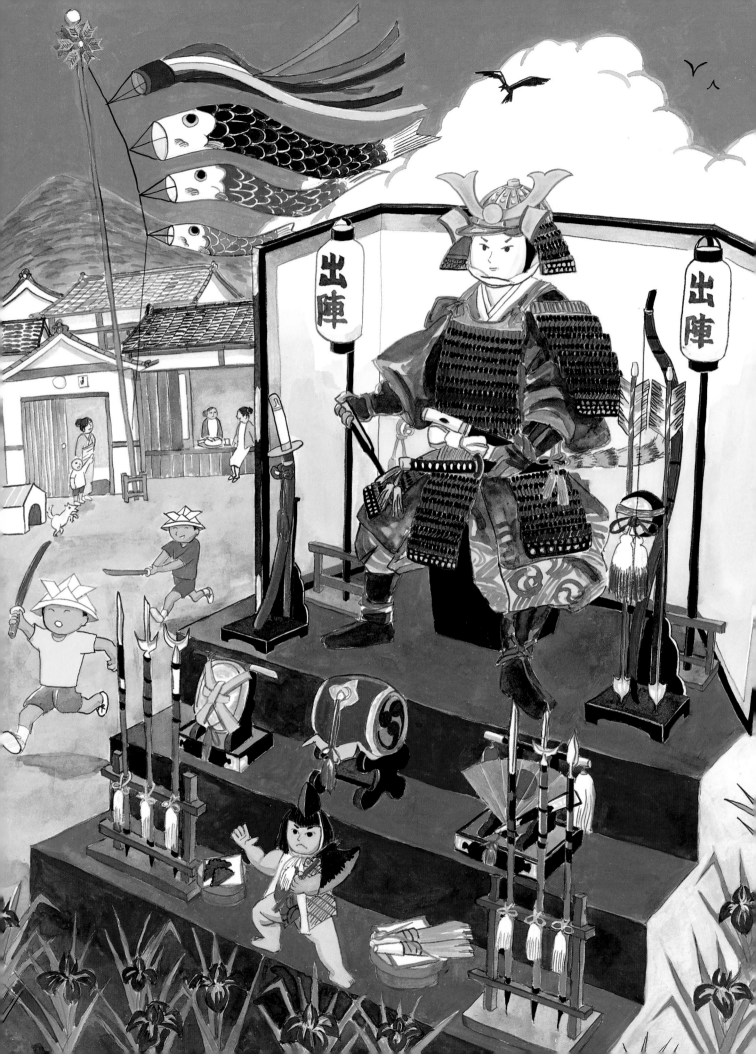

Kodomo no Hi

Children's Day

*In ancient China, people set out medicinal herbs every May 5 to ward off disease. When this idea arrived in Japan, people used **shobu** (iris) because they believed iris kept away evil. Later, in the Middle Ages, boys were given kites with pictures of warriors and carp streamers. The festival came to be known as **Tango no Sekku** (Boys' Day). Some people still celebrate it as Iris Day. In 1948, this festival was made a national holiday, celebrating both boys and girls.*

What are all these fish-shaped banners flying outside of homes? Red and black, some small and some more than 15 feet long. Count them and you will know how many sons there are in the family. The biggest **koi nobori** (carp banner) is for the eldest son. When a baby boy is born in Japan, his parents buy a paper or cloth **koi** to fly on May 5.

Why carp? Because families want their sons to be as tough as koi. Like old-time **samurai**, koi fear nothing, swim upstream, and never give up! Red is for the sun and black for rain clouds. Both help crops survive. The bright streamers on top of the poles frighten away evil spirits.

Schools are closed. Families pack their **bento** (lunch boxes) and head off to parks. Later, children and parents will crowd into the sports stadium. They'll cheer for their favorite **sumo** wrestlers and marvel at the swift slash of the **kendo** fighters' bamboo swords.

Shrines, stores, and homes are decorated with iris, a flower that stands straight on its stem like a samurai sword. Symbols of strength like iris and koi reflect parents' hopes that their children grow up strong and healthy.

At home, some parents of sons display on stands tiny samurai warrior swords, daggers, bows and arrows, armor, fans, and a white horse, the sign of courage and strength. Some include a clay figure of Kintaro, the Golden Boy, who was raised by Yamauba, the mountain witch. He never grew older and was strong enough to wrestle bears! And the spirits of samurai? They are not forgotten, not even in modern Japan. A tray with rice dumplings, sweets, and **sake** (rice wine) has been prepared for them.

こいのぼり

Koi Nobori
Carp Banner

The Shogun

The **Kodomo no Hi** festival usually includes exhibitions of traditional Japanese sports and martial arts. Sumo is especially popular. The sport began more than 1,500 years ago, and **rikishi**, "gentlemen of strength" (sumo wrestlers), are heroes to Japanese children, like baseball stars are to Americans.

The rules are simple: two rikishi fight in a 15-foot-wide ring. The winner is the one who knocks the other out of the ring. No punching or kicking is allowed. Sumo wrestlers can push, slap, trip, and flip. Most matches last less than a minute. Wrestlers must be huge to be good at sumo. Some weigh more than 400 pounds! Boys usually start training for sumo when they are 15 years old.

The Yamato did not remain the most powerful clan in Japan. Other warlords banded together and began to control large parts of the country. In 1185, Yoritomo became the top military leader of Japan. In 1192 the emperor gave him the title of **shogun**, which is short for words meaning: "barbarian-subduing great general." His military government was called a shogunate. After Yoritomo died, other military governors became shogun.

For the next 700 years, the Japanese people would be ruled by military leaders. The shogun made the laws, collected taxes, built roads, and tried to keep other powerful families from gaining control. The emperor had no real political or military power, but cultural activities—art, music, writing—flourished at his court.

There was no peace in Japan under the shogun. Warlords lived in huge castles surrounded by moats and fought each other. Their soldiers were called samurai, which means "those who serve." At first, samurai were just farmers who fought when ordered. Eventually, the samurai developed their own strict code of behavior, called **Bushido**, The Way of the Warrior. Above all came loyalty to the lord. Samurai had to be very brave. They could not show pain, anger or despair. Every samurai carried a short dagger and a long curved sword. Nobody else in Japan was allowed to have weapons.

Japanese society under the nobility was divided into four classes; the samurai were the highest, then came the farmers. Under them were the craftsmen, and last were the merchants. The farmers worked very hard, owned no land, and paid high taxes. They were important, but only because they produced food and raised livestock. The craftsmen who made pottery, woven fabrics, furniture, metalware, and jewelry earned very little and had hard lives. The merchants were despised as parasites, but some became very rich.

Counting in Japanese

In Japanese, August is called **Hachigatsu**, which means eighth month. If you know how to count to 12, you can name all the months of the year. Just add **gatsu** (month) to the number. Here is how to count in Japanese:

ichi,	ni,	san,	shi,	go,	roku,
1,	2,	3,	4,	5,	6,

shichi,	hachi,	ku,	ju,	juichi,	juni
7,	8,	9,	10,	11,	12

Koi Nobori—Carp Streamers

A koi nobori is made of two pieces of fabric cut out in the shape of a fish, then sewn together leaving the mouth end open. When the koi is hung on a pole outside, the breeze blows into its mouth and the koi moves like a live fish.

Here's how to make one from paper.

You will need poster paint or markers; tissue paper or some facial tissues; string; a dowel or stick; and about 3 feet by 3 feet of kraft or butcher paper. (Or use large paper grocery bags, cut open.)

Fold the paper in half and staple corners. Draw a carp-shaped fish and cut it out (you will get two identical fish). Staple or glue koi edges, leaving open a big mouth. Paint or color both sides and let dry. Stuff crumpled tissue through the mouth of the fish so it puffs. Tie a string bridle to the mouth and hang the carp on a pole.

If you want to make one to fly outside, skip the tissue. Instead, fold the open mouth-edges over a circle of light wire and glue them so the mouth stays open, as in the diagram. Tie string to the wire, and hang on a pole or broomstick outside in the wind.

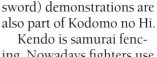

Kendo (the way of the sword) demonstrations are also part of Kodomo no Hi.

Kendo is samurai fencing. Nowadays fighters use sabers of bamboo, not metal. They wear protective costumes: a helmet with a cage for the face, leather, and padding for the body. Their feet are hidden by a long split skirt, so the "enemy" cannot guess the next move. Both men and women learn kendo.

Hina Matsuri

Dolls' Festival—March 3

*Japanese girls look forward eagerly to **Hina Matsuri**, also called Girls' Day, when families display dolls of the emperor and empress with their court. In the past, farmers would purify themselves at the beginning of March before planting rice. They believed the way to do it was to transfer their impurity to paper dolls. Then they floated the dolls away down a river. In the seventeenth century, Japan began to produce well-made dolls. The custom gradually changed to a display of dolls representing the imperial court. Some people still float paper dolls.*

"Now be gentle! You are not to play with these dolls. Just look at them!"

For the past week, grandmothers, mothers, and daughters have been unpacking boxes and unwrapping tissue paper. At last, after one long year, girls can see their **hina** dolls again.

All over Japan young girls invite their friends to tea. The girls come in their brightest spring kimono held with their fanciest **obi** sash. In their hair they wear bows, flowers, and tinkling bells. The hostess bows politely to greet the guests, and the guests bow back. Then everyone kneels on cushions at a low table. Daintily, they sip green tea and eat pink and white rice cakes. They giggle, chat, and admire the hina. Of course they feel very important. This is their special day!

After two or three weeks, mothers and daughters carefully repack each doll and store it. The girls sadly tell their hina good-by until next March.

The dolls are dressed in costumes of the Middle Ages. The emperor and empress dolls reign on the top step of a tiered stand. The empress wears a gorgeous silk kimono. Other hina represent ladies-in-waiting, courtiers, musicians, singers, and servants. There is also a toy household with miniature dishes, bowls, chopsticks, and tiny furniture.

Hina are expensive. They are passed on from great-grandmothers, grandmothers, and mothers. They are a family treasure. Many women take their dolls with them when they get married. They save them for their future children.

**Hina Matsuri
Dolls' Festival**

Japan Shuts Its Door

In shogun times, women lost status and rights. Customs changed. Only the eldest son inherited the family farm or fortune. Fathers ordered daughters whom to marry. Husbands and fathers decided what women and girls should do. Women ate after men had finished. They went into the furo after men were done. But samurai women were allowed to act like samurai. They learned warrior skills and were expected to use them.

In 1543, a wild storm at sea blew a Portuguese trading ship to the shores of Japan. The traders soon sold all their merchandise, bought Japanese goods, and returned home. They made a large profit. The news spread and other Portuguese traders sailed to Japan. Along with other goods, they sold guns and ammunition. In 1549 a Catholic priest, Francis Xavier, brought the Christian religion to Japan. More than 300,000 Japanese became Christians.

Meanwhile, one shogun family, the Tokugawa, was becoming very powerful. It forced the other rich families to spend their time and money on roadbuilding and other useful improvements. There was peace, but the shogun worried about what the Europeans were up to. The Tokugawa believed that the Christian religion was a danger to Shinto and Japanese traditions, that Christians would try to gain political power. Christians were persecuted and killed. Foreign missionaries were expelled.

In 1639, after Christians rebelled, the Tokugawa excluded all Europeans from Japan.

All trade with foreign countries was stopped, except for that with China and Holland. New laws forbade Japanese to leave Japan. Anyone caught trying to do so was executed. For the next 225 years Japan's door to most of the outside world was locked.

Japanese Houses

Traditional Japanese houses are made of wood. Sliding doors separate the rooms. The floor is covered with woven straw mats called **tatami**. Low tables for eating and writing and small chests are the only furniture. A special alcove in the main room provides space for a prized painting, a flower arrangement, or another family treasure. At night, thick pads called **futon** are pulled out of closets and spread on the tatami, for sleeping. Meals are prepared in small, simple kitchens in the back of the house.

It is very rude to step on tatami with shoes. Japanese people take off their shoes and put on slippers when entering a house. Today, many Japanese live in Western-style homes, with Western furniture and modern kitchens. But they still like to have one traditional tatami room where they relax and entertain guests.

Kimono

Even today, Japanese women like to wear kimono for special occasions such as festivals and weddings. Kimono are robes with long, wide sleeves, usually of silk. They are wrapped around the body and held closed with long, wide sashes called obi. An elaborate formal kimono may have many layers, each of a different color or pattern. The obi is tied at the back in a large, intricate knot with many folds. Kimono are beautiful and graceful to look at but the elaborate ones are heavy, hot, and hard to put on and wear! **Yukata** are summer kimonos. They're usually made of cotton, and tied with a simple sash.

Haiku

A **haiku** is a short poem with three lines, with a pattern of five, then seven, then five syllables. Japanese poets created this style during the seventeenth and eighteenth centuries, and their poetry and its style are still popular today. Haiku were generally based on nature, or used at least one word that referred to a season. Haiku seem simple but are not. They make people think and search for different meanings. Here is one:

A-ma-ga-e-ru	A little frog
Ba-sho-u-ni no-ri-te.	Riding on a banana leaf
So-yo-gi ke-ri	Trembling

あまがえる
ばしょうにのりて
そよぎけり

Mibu Ohana Taue

The Rice God Festival

Ohana means flower, **taue**-means rice-planting. The flower-hat dance was first performed to chase away rice-eating worms. Later it became part of **Ohana Taue**.

Growing paddy rice requires teamwork and cooperation. Since ancient times, Japanese men have prepared the fields and women have planted.

In 1578, in the town of Mibu (now called Chiyoda), a Japanese warlord decided to trick his enemy. He ordered his toughest soldiers to disguise themselves as dancers wearing silk robes and flower-decorated hats. When the "dancers" entered their enemy's castle, off came the clothes that hid their armor. Swords flashed in the sun and the battle was won. To mark this victory, the warlord held a festival, **Ohana Taue**, *for rice-planting farmers.*

Ohana Taue is still celebrated on the first Sunday of June, after the end of the rainy season. On this date, Chiyoda farmers believe, the Rice God comes down from his high mountain to bless their crops. They all pray for his visit. In the fields, they burn heaps of rice straw, so the flames can carry their message to him:

"Welcome! Welcome! Rice God! Bring us good crops!"

Music is everywhere: drums, flutes, bamboo clackers, and voices. Women in white and blue yukata dance in the streets. Their hats support garlands of white paper flowers like graceful parasols. Even the black oxen have been dressed up. They wear gold saddles on their backs, bright ribbons on their horns, and carry silk banners with the names of their owners. Oxen, musicians, dancers, and singers all walk down the main street to the rice fields. Excited crowds cheer them on. The sun is high. It's hot, and humid. But who cares?

In the rice paddies, ropes have been stretched across the fields to mark straight rows for planting seedlings. Women farmers stand in a long row, waiting for the sign to start working. Is the Rice God hovering there in the air? Has he brought his blessings? The dance leader chants:

"Plant your rice in a row. Don't miss a single sprout."

Other singers take up the refrain. In one movement, all the women bend down and plant a row of rice sprouts. They straighten, step back, bend, plant, again and again. Row upon row. Soon small emerald-green sprouts fill the whole paddy.

The festival continues. People sing, dance, and buy snacks and drinks from vendors. Children play games. At dusk, the celebrations stop. The Rice God flies back to his mountain to stay until next summer. "Please remember to return!" people beg.

At home, farmers offer the Rice God food, drinks, and flowers on their family altars. They hope their crops will be safe, that it will rain enough but not too much, that storms will not blow away the tender seedlings. Will the god bless their crops this year?

Oshogatsu

New Year's Festival

Modern Japan adopted the Western calendar in 1873. So the New Year—Japan's most important holiday—is now celebrated on January 1. It is a national holiday. Offices and factories are closed, but unlike Western countries, Oshogatsu is not a time for partying. It is a family festival.

Kids are laughing, giggling, clapping, shouting: "Higher! No! Lower! More to the right! Now to the left!" What's going on? It's **fuku warai,** a favorite New Year's game. Someone has drawn the outline of a huge face on a large piece of paper and put it on the tatami. But the face has no features. A blindfolded boy is putting paper cutouts of a nose, a mouth, and eyes on it. But the boy is guessing the places all wrong. His friends are trying to help him. Everyone is yelling at the same time. "Okay, Okay. I'm done," he says. He takes off his blindfold and has to laugh at the face he has made. The mouth is under the chin, one eye is up and the other way down. The nose is on the edge of the paper, almost falling off the cheek.

On New Year's Day many people like to wake up at dawn to see the first sunrise of the year. Before breakfast, everyone lights candles and incense at the family altar. Parents and children wish each other:

"Akemashite Omedeto Gozaimasu," Happy New Year!

Together, they sip sweet spiced rice wine.

After, many families will put on their best clothes to make their first visit of the year to a shrine to post a wish for the New Year.

It's a wonderful festival for children! Parents, grandparents, aunts and uncles give them **otoshidama,** special envelopes with gifts of money. There are games with special New Year bats and shuttlecocks, and kites to fly. Some children hold kites larger than themselves. Many kites have a ribbon of thin bone at the bottom that makes a loud humming noise when the wind blows through it. *Z-m-m-m!*

When it's time to go home, there's fuku warai, card games, visiting with relatives, and, of course, eating!

**Akemashite Omedeto
Happy New Year**

31

Preparing for the New Year

Today many Japanese Americans can recall family stories of how grandparents who worked on Hawaiian sugar cane plantations celebrated the New Year with community **mochi**-pounding. And how, even during the bleak time of internment during World War II, families organized mochi-pounding to bring in a new year.

In Tokyo in late December, millions of people visit neighborhood shrines. Stalls set up at the shrines sell candles and incense sticks for family altars, bamboo and pine trees, fern and woven rice-straw ropes.

Want to keep away evil spirits? Place a bamboo and a pine on each side of your house entrance. Want a long healthy life and a good marriage? Hang rice straw ropes and fern above the door, tuck in an orange, a persimmon, a paper lobster, and seaweed.

Two or three days before January 1, homes are cleaned. Meals are cooked, enough to last three days. The wives and mothers want to be free to enjoy New Year with their families.

Finally, it's New Year's Eve. For dinner, there are special buckwheat noodles—extra long, so everyone can live a long, long life. After dinner, adults visit and watch the annual New Year's special on TV, and children try to stay awake until midnight. Shortly before midnight people will gather near Buddhist temples and parks, and stand quietly in the frosty night.

At midnight the first temple bell sounds. The bell ringers wait until each sound dies completely before striking again. The bells will ring 108 times. It takes about an hour. To Buddhists, the number 108 stands for the number of "passions and delusions" that humans must rid themselves of. If you can't go out, you can listen to radio and TV broadcasts of the ringing from famous temples.

Mochi

New Year foods include sweet black beans, dried fish, mashed sweet potato with chestnuts, yams, and herring roe (herring eggs). But the most important holiday food is **mochi**. Mochi are round cakes made of sweet (glutinous) rice which has been steamed and pounded. Japanese eat mochi on at least the first three days of New Year. They slice them and add them to special soups. Families display tiered **kagamimochi** in the living room alcove.

Every grocery store sells mochi but some Japanese like the old tradition of pounding rice at home. It is hard work but fun to do with the whole family. **Mochitsuki** (preparing mochi) is one of the ceremonial customs of Shinto. Often, professional mochi pounders put on a show. They dance around a huge pot as they crush lots of rice into paste. Their arms bulge as they bang in rhythm.

Japanese Food

Japanese people cook food quickly in order to keep its natural flavors and nutrition. Textures and colors are important. Traditional Japanese foods are those from the ocean—fish, seaweed—and rice, vegetables, and foods made from soybeans. **Tempura** is batter-dipped, deep-fried seafood, fish, and vegetables. The Japanese learned this technique from the Portuguese. Noodles (**udon** and **soba**) of wheat or buckwheat came from China.

Today, Japanese grocery stores stock a large variety of frozen and pre-cooked foods. People eat more meat than they used to, although it's very expensive. Many Japanese enjoy American-style cereals, ice cream, and sodas. Fast food chains sell familiar American brands of hamburgers and chicken.

New Year celebrations continue during the week. On January 6, firemen in 400-year old costumes greet the New Year with terrifying stunts on giant ladders. (Firemen have been important in Japan since medieval times. Traditional wooden houses, with their tatami floors and paper **shoji** doors caught fire easily, and the fires could quickly engulf whole neighborhoods.)

Cold Noodles

*A quick, simple meal or snack in Japan is likely to be noodles. Japanese people like both hot and cold noodle dishes. Most recipes depend on **dashi** (a mild-flavored soup stock) for their special taste. Dashi is commonly available in packets in supermarkets that carry some Asian foods. Just add water. **Mirin** (sweet rice wine) comes in small bottles. This recipe serves 4.*

Noodles: 1 package dried soba (buckwheat) or somen (thin wheat) noodles

Bring lots of water to boil in big pot, add noodles. Cook until done but not mushy. Time (between 2 and 10 minutes) depends on thickness of noodle. Pour noodles carefully into a colander. Run cold water over them until they are cool. Drain.

Sauce: 1 cup prepared dashi, 2 tablespoons mirin, 2 tablespoons soy sauce, ¼ teaspoon sugar.

Mix all the above together in a small pan. Heat just to boiling. Remove from stove and cool.

Condiments: (your choice, pick several): 2 finely chopped green onions, 2 tablespoons sesame seeds, toasted (see onigiri recipe, page 11); 2 sheets nori, toasted over low heat, snipped with scissors into small bits.

1 teaspoon wasabi (horseradish—very pungent!) powder, mixed with water to make a thick paste, or 3 tablespoons grated fresh ginger.

To serve: Pour the dipping sauce into 4 small bowls. Place condiments on 4 small plates. Divide noodles into 4 shallow bowls. Each person can mix condiments into their sauce, or sprinkle on their noodles. To eat, pick up some noodles with your hashi (or fork), dunk them into the sauce, and eat. Slurping is fine!

U.S. Ships Come to Japan

After 1872, news of Western progress spread quickly. All over Japan, as children bounced balls, they chanted the "10 desirable Western things":

gas lamps
steam engines
horse-drawn carriages
cameras
telegraphs
lightning rods
newspapers
schools
post-offices
steamboats

In 1853, U.S. Navy Commodore Matthew Perry sailed to Japan with four ships. On the decks were big cannons. Commodore Perry's mission was to make Japan open its ports for trade. The Japanese, observing British successes at colonizing China knew they could not win a fight against powerful new American weapons. The shogun signed a treaty with the United States and soon after, with Great Britain, Russia, and Holland.

Japan had opened its door, but most Japanese were unhappy. They thought that the treaties gave too many advantages to Western countries. They called them "Unequal Treaties."

The shogunate was in trouble. Rich merchants opposed them. Natural disasters, famines, and taxes caused farmers to rebel. Other powerful families joined together against the shogun. Under such pressure, in 1868 the last shogun resigned. Power was once again in the hands of the emperor and his supporters.

The new emperor, Meiji, supported traditional art, music, and writing, but he also wanted Japan to learn from the West. Japanese were encouraged to sign on with American labor contractors seeking farm workers for Hawaiian plantations. The emperor sent a Japanese delegation to San Francisco in 1872, and the following year to Europe. When they returned, they reported on Western progress.

Fuku Warai

Make your own fuku warai game. Draw a big face, like this one, on a large sheet of paper. Draw and cut out eyes, nose, ears, mouth. Find a scarf to use for a blindfold, and play.

One Hundred Waka

Waka are short, five-line poems. The style originated in the eighth century, and scribes and officials gained fame if they were skillful at writing waka. Later, people played games where each person would compose two or three lines of the poem. Today it is customary for the emperor and empress to write waka at the New Year. At New Year, some people play Japan's oldest card game, called: "One Hundred Waka." Someone is chosen to read the first half of a poem. Cards with the second half of different waka are spread out on the floor. Everyone hunts for the matching one. The first person to find it is the winner. Some people can guess the rest of the waka after hearing just one or two syllables!

Menko

Menko first appeared in the 1700s. They were made of clay, wood, or lead with pictures of animals or people. In the 1890s the Japanese began to manufacture cardboard menko. These had pictures of famous warriors or politicians. Today menko cards show famous athletes, movie stars, and cartoon characters. They come in a variety of shapes and are sold in boxes. Some people collect menko cards. Old ones are very expensive.

Two or more children can play the menko game. Children sometimes organize teams to compete against each other.

To make your own menko cards, cut thick cardboard in rectangles of 2″ × 2½″. Leave one side plain and decorate the other with drawings, or colors, or stickers. Make 20 cards, or more if you wish. The game has many variations.

Here is one way to play. Scatter the cards on the floor or flat ground with the plain side facing downwards. Each person should choose one menko with which to play. Take turns trying to flip over a card on the ground by hitting its side sharply with your own menko. If the card on the ground flips, keep it. The one who flips the most cards is the winner.

Some kids like to play menko another way. They draw a ring on the ground and try to knock their "enemy's" card out of it, like in sumo wrestling.

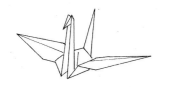

Yuki Matsuri

The Sapporo Snow Festival

*Ice-skating was introduced in Hokkaido in 1877. As time went by, making snow and ice sculptures for the enjoyment of gliding skaters became a winter tradition. Sapporo has held a snow festival since 1950. It outdid itself for the 1972 Winter Olympic Games, the first in Japan. Now the Sapporo **Yuki Matsuri** is a world-famous yearly event.*

It is February in Sapporo, the largest city in Hokkaido, Japan's northern island. The weather is freezing, 22 degrees. The air is clear and crisp. Odori Park is crowded with visitors. They are here for the Snow Festival. Two million people come every winter.

Weeks before the festival, snow is hauled in from the mountains and piled in Odori Park. It's a lot of snow, almost 40,000 tons. It takes about 250 trucks and 7,600 trips to bring it. Dozens of volunteers form the snow into huge blocks and spray them with water that quickly turns into ice. The frozen blocks become carving material for talented sculptors.

It's a magical sight, especially at night. In the moonlight, an ice shogun castle shimmers. Children rush here and there. What should they look at first? The life-size white snow horse, the dragon with scales and twisted tail, the characters from TV and movies? Surely ancient spirits are flitting among the translucent carvings. Yum! the delicious smell of roasting chestnuts! "Quick, Mom, buy me some! I'm starving!" What fun! Noses are frozen, feet are cold in spite of heavy socks and boots, but **shikata ga nai**, it can't be helped.

"Shikata ga nai" are words people often say in Japan. Lights suddenly go out, a car stalls, the typhoon blows off a roof—"Shikata ga nai!" It can't be helped! Even strangers in Japan soon learn to not get angry at difficulties they can't avoid and say, "Shikata ga nai!"

Yuki Matsuri
Snow Festival

The Military Lead Japan to War

Each year on August 6 and August 9, sirens blare in Hiroshima and Nagasaki, at the exact time when the atom bombs were dropped. All over Japan people stop whatever they are doing, bow their heads and say a silent prayer. Victims of war are remembered in memorial services. People pray for a peaceful world free of nuclear weapons.

Japan modernized rapidly. But it lacked raw material for its industry. Ambitious military leaders thought Japan, not Europe, should rule Asia. In 1931, the Japanese army attacked Manchuria and China. The Chinese fought back, but Japan eventually gained control of much of China. England, France, and other European countries, threatened in Europe by Nazi Germany, could not defend their Asian interests from the Japanese. The fighting spread. The Japanese army was fierce and relentless.

In December 1941, Japan attacked the U.S. naval base at Pearl Harbor in Hawaii. The United States entered the war. The fighting intensified. Cities in Asia were destroyed. Millions died. Japan controlled most of East Asia. But after many battles, the territory Japan had taken was liberated. Then the war came to Japan. The United States fire-bombed Tokyo, killing 100,000. In August 1945, the United States dropped atomic bombs on the Japanese cities of Hiroshima and Nagasaki. Faced with the overwhelming devastation of these weapons, Japan surrendered. The war ended. Almost two million Japanese had died. Their country was in ruins. U.S. troops and authorities took over Japan.

U.S. authorities governed the country and helped it recover from the disasters of war. Emperor Hirohito declared that he was no longer a god. By May 3, 1947, Japan had a new constitution, written mainly by the United States. Japan became a democracy. A Bill of Rights now protected the Japanese people. They became equal under the law, could vote, join any political party, practice any religion, and have free education. In the constitution Japan renounced war forever. The Japanese people rebuilt quickly. Within 20 years, Japan was producing what the world wanted to buy and becoming a prosperous modern nation.

Modern Japan

The Bill of Rights of 1947 changed life in Japan, especially for women. Now the law allows them to vote, to have their own property and to get an equal share of the family inheritance. They choose who to marry and can apply for divorce if they wish. They share equal responsibility for the children with their husband. April 10 is now Women's Rights Day.

Girls and boys go to school from the age of 6 to 15, and learn the same subjects. Public schools and textbooks are free; 95% of girls graduate from high school and 45% go on to college.

Japanese people are well informed and love to read. Every day, more than 40 million newspapers are sold. Japan is fourth in the world in the number of new books published every year. Almost everyone has a radio and TV. Many people complain that they know more about the rest of the world than the rest of the world knows about Japan.

Before World War II, modern products from Japanese factories were of low quality, compared with those made in Europe and the United States. The workers were badly paid. Today Japanese products are among the best in the world, famous for their high quality, advanced design and style. Workers have strong unions, and working conditions are much better.

Employees get livable salaries and many benefits. Health insurance is cheap. Children get regular free health checks at school. Today, people can enjoy their leisure time. Millions travel in their own country and abroad.

Because of good health care and a better diet since the war's end in 1945, young Japanese people are now about two inches taller than in the past. And they can expect to live long lives. Life expectancy for women in Japan is 84 years and for men 77. In 1968, the Japanese government, recognizing that there are now many more old people than before, made **Keiro no Hi** (Respect for Aged Day), September 15, a national holiday. Schools are closed, and it's a nice time for children to visit the senior members of their families, bring a gift and show their gratitude and appreciation for the elder generation.

Today Japanese people worry about modern problems: overcrowding, waste, pollution, careless use of natural resources, neglect of the environment. Huge amounts of home and factory garbage pollute Japan's rivers, lakes, and harbors. Car exhaust and smoke dirty the air. More than 30 million people live in Tokyo and its surroundings. In Japanese cities, subways and commuter trains are jammed. Rush hour is called "transportation hell." Uniformed attendants help squeeze commuters into trains. On the road, traffic moves very slowly.

Origami

Origami is the art of folding paper to create animals, birds, flowers, and other shapes. The paper must not be cut so as not to hurt the spirit of the paper!

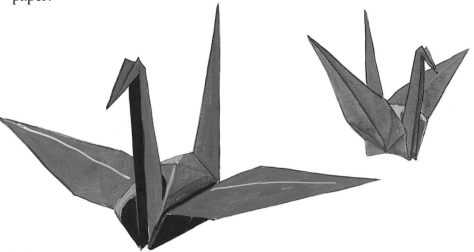

Tsuru, the Mysterious Stranger

*Japanese love the **tsuru** (crane), a magnificent red-crested white bird. Its black-tipped wings spread 5 feet. To Japanese, as well as Chinese and Koreans, cranes stand for peace and long life. Today these cranes are very rare and in danger of disappearing. Most are migratory. About 200 live year-round in Japan, on Hokkaido, where they receive special protection.*

The story of Tsuru tells about sacrifice in return for a good deed. It is very important in Japan to show gratitude and appreciate kindness.

It was a cold, snowy, stormy night. In a tiny village, a man was eating his last bowl of rice. Everything was silent. Suddenly the man heard a tapping on his front door. There stood a pale young woman in a long kimono. As she bowed she whispered: "I am freezing!"

"**Dozo ohairi kudasai!** Please come in," the kind villager said. He invited her to sit on a cushion near the fire and share his meal.

After the woman had eaten and rested, she wanted to leave but the man said:

"Don't go out again in this terrible snowstorm. Stay here. You can have my mother's room. She died last year."

In the morning, the guest gave the villager a beautiful piece of cloth: brilliant white with some tiny black and red specks. It felt soft, smooth, and warm.

"I used your mother's loom," the stranger said. "I didn't want to wake

you to ask for permission. Please sell this cloth. This is the only way I can repay your great kindness."

The villager easily sold the cloth for a good price and the woman told him she would weave some more, but she added:

"Please never try to watch me at the loom. My work is my secret."

The snow continued. The woman stayed in the hut. She hardly ate, just worked and worked at the loom.

"Who is she?" the villager wondered. "Where does she get the thread to weave?" Curious, he peeked one night into her room and gasped: at the loom sat a white crane painfully plucking out her feathers, which she wove into a cloth. Suddenly the crane turned her head and said in the woman's voice:

"Oh, you found out my secret! My feathers were all I had to give you! Alas, now I must leave forever!"

Then she disappeared. The man ran out the door to look where she had gone. Far away, in the thick falling snow he thought he could make out a flying crane.

Sakura Matsuri

The Cherry Blossom Festival

*In Japan, in the spring, everyone tries to make time for **hanami**, cherry blossom viewing. Thousands of Japanese picnic under **sakura** (cherry) trees. Companies reserve space in parks for office outings. People eat, drink, and sing.*

Clouds of pink paper flowers drift through trees. The smoky aroma of **yakitori** (grilled meat on skewers) greets visitors. Food stalls tempt with **soba** noodles, vegetables fried in tempura batter, **anpan** buns stuffed with sweet red bean paste, rice-cakes colored pink, white, and green. It's **Sakura Matsuri**, the Cherry Blossom Festival.

Is this festival in Japan? No. It is in the United States. In San Francisco, Los Angeles, Seattle, Washington, D.C., and other cities, Japanese Americans have created a new tradition for celebrating their heritage.

Want to make a paper frog that opens and shuts its mouth? Go to the origami corner. Like fishing? Grab a net and try to catch a goldfish as it darts away in a big tank. Enjoy dancing? Music? There's sure to be taiko drumming, and classical Japanese music. Listen to the **shamisen** (three-string banjo), and the **koto** (13-string harp). Meet a master calligrapher. There are displays of **ikebana** and **bonsai**, and brush paintings. Story-tellers entertain children with folktales about bravery, honor, and loyalty. And, if the festival is in a Buddhist temple, there will surely be a tatami room for **cha no yu**, the tea ceremony.

Many people help to make the festival a success. Community groups organized volunteers to make and sell food. Children from dance groups have practiced for weeks. Candidates for Cherry Blossom Queen will be there, dressed in their beautiful kimonos. There may be a kite-flying contest. Taiko drummer groups and **karate** students from all over will perform on stage. Local officials and well-known people will show up. There may be special guests, visitors from Japan. There will probably be a parade, with drummers, dancers, and a mikoshi (portable shrine). The festival will last a weekend, or maybe two. Thousands will come. Everyone is invited, to have fun and learn about Japanese culture, to honor the heritage of more than 848,000 Japanese Americans. You will be welcome to join in!

**Sakura Matsuri
Cherry Blossom Festival**

Japanese in America

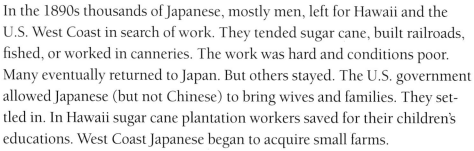

Bonsai is the art of growing dwarf trees. Young trees are pruned, trained, and grown in tiny pots. Eventually they become beautiful miniature trees. Some are 100 years old.

In the 1890s thousands of Japanese, mostly men, left for Hawaii and the U.S. West Coast in search of work. They tended sugar cane, built railroads, fished, or worked in canneries. The work was hard and conditions poor. Many eventually returned to Japan. But others stayed. The U.S. government allowed Japanese (but not Chinese) to bring wives and families. They settled in. In Hawaii sugar cane plantation workers saved for their children's educations. West Coast Japanese began to acquire small farms.

When times got harder, American workers began to worry that immigrants would take their jobs. Landowners and farmers resented Japanese farmers. In 1913, a California law forbade Japanese from buying land. They could only lease it for three years, and couldn't pass it on to their families. In 1924 a new U.S. law stopped all immigration from Asia. Only Japanese born in the United States could become citizens. By 1940 more than 60% of Japanese in the United States were American-born. The 90,000 Japanese in California were less than one percent of the state's population.

The Sakura Song

Washington D.C.'s famous cherry trees were gifts from the Japanese government in 1912. Cuttings from these trees were sent back to Japan in 1952 to help restore war-damaged cherry groves.

Many Japanese Americans keep the custom of sakura viewing. Some families and community groups have developed their own custom of viewing local wild flowers in the spring. Whether you are viewing sakura, or lupines and poppies, it is a reminder that this world is changeable and impermanent.

Sakura, sakura	Oh, cherry blossoms, cherry blossoms,
Yayoi no sorawa	The March sky is filled with blooming cherry blossoms.
Miwatasu kagiri	As far as you can see,
Kasumi ka kumo ka	They look like mist or a cloud.
Nioizo izuru	Fragrance is floating in the air.
Izaya, izaya	Let's go, let's go
Miniyukan	To see them.

Internment

After Japan bombed Pearl Harbor, many newspapers wrote that Japanese in the United States were traitors and spies. The military worried they would help Japan if it invaded. On February 19, 1942, President Franklin Roosevelt ordered all 120,000 persons of Japanese ancestry to be removed from the West Coast. Men, women, and children were to be sent to special internment camps. They could bring only what they could carry. Those who refused to go were arrested. More than two thirds were citizens, born in the United States.

Japanese-American neighborhoods in Seattle, San Francisco, and Los Angeles became ghost towns. The ten camps, in isolated parts of the West and South, were surrounded by barbed wire and guard towers. Living conditions were terrible. The people were prisoners.

In Hawaii, it was different. There were 158,000 Japanese Americans, a third of the population. They were badly needed, as workers and customers. Local authorities ignored the internment order.

In 1943, the United States agreed to allow Japanese Americans to join the U.S. military. About 20,000 served courageously. Most fought in segregated units in Europe and North Africa. But many Japanese Americans refused to serve until their own people were released from the camps.

When it became clear that Japan would lose the war, the internees were released. Most had lost everything: homes, furniture, mementos, cars, farms, businesses. They started over. It would be more than 40 years before the U.S. government apologized and 50 years before the government paid them any compensation for what they lost.

In the 1950s new laws opened U.S. immigration to Japanese. Immigrants could become citizens. The civil rights movement of the 1960s opened more doors. People of Japanese heritage joined mainstream American life.

For Japanese Americans, February 19 is Day of Remembrance. It's a day for young and old to talk about the history of the Japanese in America, and to remind everyone of the importance of protecting the basic rights of all citizens.

Ikebana is a special way of arranging flowers: a tall stem stands for heaven, a lower one for mankind, and the shortest for earth. Shapes and lines are more important than color.

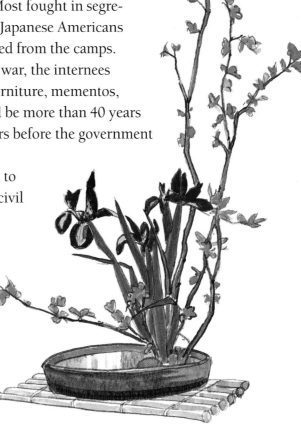

The Three Tengu and Tanuki

Sake made of fermented rice is the "wine of Japan." People drink it cold or warm at festivals, weddings, parties, and other important occasions. Sake is also used in cooking. It gives a special flavor to soups and sauces.

*Not too long ago, before TV, candy sellers would come to every neighborhood in Tokyo. They were called **kamishibaiya-san** which means "paper theater men." Children would run with their money to buy candy. Then they'd listen to the stories told by the kamishibaiya, who carried a wooden-framed box like a stage. Inside were picture boards which they pulled out as they told the story. Kamishibaiya-san acted out all the characters.*

The **Tengu** are long-nosed mischievous goblins who live in the mountains. Some look almost human and wear little round caps on their heads, others have beaks, feathers, and claws. They are all naughty but not too smart.

Three Tengu were sitting on a rock and took turns waving a magic paper fan. When they used one side of the fan, their long noses grew longer. When they waved the other, their noses became shorter. Oh how they laughed as they looked at each other. "Longer! Longer! Huge! Shorter! Tiny!"

Mischievous Tanuki, the badger, was watching them from behind a tree. He knew magic tricks and could make himself into anything he wanted to be.

"What a fun fan!" he thought. "I will steal it from the silly Tengu."

At once, Tanuki changed himself into a little girl holding a plate with four **anpan** (buns filled with red bean paste)—the Tengu's favorite food. As soon as the three Tengu saw the anpan, they rushed up to grab them. But, with four buns and three Tengu, who would get the extra one?

The Tengu argued and argued.

"Stop! Don't quarrel!" the sly Tanuki told the Tengu, "Each take one bun. Leave your fan on the ground. Close your eyes and hold your breath. The last bun is a prize for the one who holds his breath longest. Start at the count of three."

The silly Tengu agreed at once and Tanuki started:

"Ichi, ni . . ." but before saying "san," he pounced on the fan and fled.

Tanuki ran and ran until he came to a castle. A beautiful princess was napping in a hammock in the garden. Tanuki crept up to her and fanned and fanned her nose. It grew longer and longer. Suddenly, the princess woke up. Her face felt heavy. Was that a hose hanging above her lips? No! It was her nose! Uttering a terrible scream she fainted.

What a commotion in the castle! Servants, soldiers, men, women, and children scurried about looking for the evil spirit that had made the princess so ugly. The shogun summoned all the wisest men, the best doctors in Japan. Alas, nobody could help.

Finally the shogun announced:

"The one who cures the princess can marry her and become a prince."

Tanuki came to the Lord and bowed. "I will make the honored princess beautiful again," he promised. Could a fat badger with a big round tummy save the princess? The shogun doubted it, but he was desperate and commanded Tanuki to try.

"My cure is secret. Nobody is allowed to watch me," said Tanuki. "Even the princess must keep her eyes closed." He tied a bandage over her eyes, and fanned her with the other side of the fan. Soon her nose became small and pretty again.

A big wedding celebration was prepared. Tanuki wandered around watching the preparations, drinking cup after cup of sake (rice wine). Soon he felt very hot and went to rest in the shade. Sleepily, he fanned himself. His nose kept growing and growing but he was too tipsy to notice. Feeling very drowsy, Tanuki leaned his head back, and enjoyed the cool breeze of the moving fan. Up, up, up went his nose right into heaven!

In heaven, the celestial workers were building a new bridge from one star to another. When they saw Tanuki's nose they were pleased. "Just the right material we need!" they cried. They pulled and pulled until they dragged sleepy Tanuki through the clouds. There he stayed.

Traditions

Nihon
Japan

The bustle of the festival seems far far away. The only sound is water boiling—Japanese call it the music of the tea kettle. People sit on tatami mats. This will not be a cooking class, but a lesson in art and behavior.

A woman in kimono gently pours boiling water over green powder tea. Then she whips the tea into a froth with a delicate bamboo brush. Her wrist, hand, and body follow ancient rules. No movement, not even the smallest one, is wasted.

When the tea is ready, everyone is asked to taste it. How bitter it is! To take away the bitterness, guests are offered small, sweet cakes.

In ancient times, cha no yu, the tea ceremony, brought calm to warriors who faced death in battle.

What does the tea ceremony teach? Patience, politeness, peace, friendship, love of beauty and harmony.

Even in modern Japan, the Japanese keep their unique perspective. As an island nation, the Japanese learned over time to cooperate, to appreciate how they were most like one another. Today, the group is still more important that the single person. People say: "No nail should stick out. It should be hammered in." They celebrate their ancient religions and their history, but new festivals celebrate modern life. Their government is a democracy, but they keep, and cherish, their emperor. They create and sell the world's most advanced technology, but honor as National Treasures the best artists and performers of their traditional culture. Foreign ideas become uniquely Japanese. Fast-food hamburgers are served with nori (seaweed), not lettuce. People leave their shoes outside their western-style homes.

Many traditions have not changed. Everyone loves festivals. And, in spite of crowding, noise, and traffic jams, there is deep respect for nature, for the seasons of the year. There is somehow time for peace and thoughtfulness.

Come visit!

Index

Kuril Islands

•Sapporo

HOKKAIDO

Aomori

Akita• •Morioka

Sado •Sendai
Yamagata
Niigata• Fukushima
HONSHU

Toyama Nagano
Kanazawa• Utsunomiya
Oki Gunto Maebashi •Mito
•Fukui Urawa
Kofu •Chiba
Tottori Gifu TOKYO •Yokohama
Matsue• Kyoto Otsu Nagoya
Kobe Tsu Shizuoka
Tsu Shima Okayama Osaka Nara
Hiroshima
Yamaguchi Takamatsu Wakayama
Fukuoka Matsuyama Tokushima
Saga Kochi
Oita *SHIKOKU*
Nagasaki• Kumamoto

Miyazaki
Kagoshima• *KYUSHU*

•Osumi Shoto

Amami O Shima Okinawa Bonin Islands
Naha•

Okinawa Gunto Sakishima Volcano Islands
•Naha Ryukyu Islands